401 ANIMAL JOKES

CANOPY
BOOKS

Designed by Deena Fleming
© 2019 by Canopy Books, LLC
13319 Poway Rd
Poway, CA

Made and Printed in USA

The animal world is packed with comedians. Furry, finned, and feathered critters are downright hilarious, and you're about to see why!

Here We Goat!

Let's kick off the silliness with some goat jokes. Get ready, because here we goat!

Q: What did one goat say to the other?

A: "You have goat to be kidding me!"

Q: Why was the barn so noisy?

A: The goats all had horns!

Q: Why are goats such bad conversationalists?

A: They're always butting in!

Q: Why did the goat join the police force?

A: He wanted to be an investigoater!

Q: Did you hear about the goat who knew martial arts?

A: He was a karate kid!

Q: What do you call a goat on a mountain?

A: A hillbilly!

Q: What's a goat's favorite instrument?

A: The tu-baa!

Q: What do you call a goat that is dressed like a clown?

A: A silly billy!

Q: What do you call a goat who brings toilet paper to the barnyard bash?

A: A party pooper!

Q: What do you call a goat's beard?

A: A goatee!

Q: Why couldn't the goat remember anything?

A: He fur-goat!

Barnyard Favorites

What do farm animals like best? Here's a roundup of their favorite things.

Q: What is a sheep's favorite newspaper?

A: The Wool Street Journal!

Q: What play do pigs like best?

A: Hamlet!

Q: What kind of cars do sheep like?

A: Lamb-borghinis!

Q: What song do goats like best?

A: "Row, Row, Row Your Goat"!

Q: What do goats like to drink?
A: Goat-orade!

Q: What is a goat's favorite TV show?
A: America's Goat Talent!

Q: What is a chicken's favorite TV show?
A: The feather forecast!

Q: What do sheep sing at birthday parties?
A: "Happy Birthday to Ewe"!

Q: What ballet do pigs like best?
A: Swine Lake!

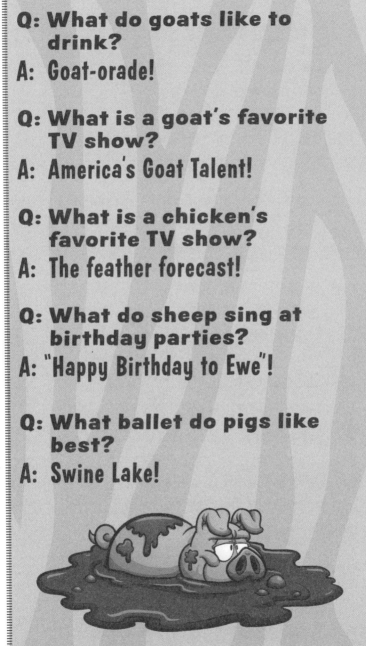

Moo!

What does the cow say? These silly puns are certain to aMOOse your friends!

Q: What do you call a cow eating your grass?

A: A lawn MOO-er!

Q: What do you call a cow that plays the trumpet?

A: A MOO-sician!

Q: What do you call a grumpy cow?

A: MOO-dy!

Q: What did one cow say to the other?

A: "MOO-ve over!"

Q: Where do cows go on field trips?

A: To the MOO-seum!

Q: How do cows hide?

A: With ca-MOO-flage!

Q: Where do cows go on Saturday night?

A: To the MOO-vies!

Q: What do you call a magician cow?

A: MOO-dini!

Q: What game do cows play at parties?

A: MOO-sical chairs!

Q: What has four legs and goes "Oom oom"?

A: A cow walking backward!

Q: What is a cow's favorite holiday?

A: Moo Year's Eve!

Q: What do cows read in the morning?

A: The MOOs-paper!

Have You Herd These?

The cows aren't quite done. Let's take one more dip into udder silliness!

Q: What do you get from a pampered cow?

A: Spoiled milk!

Q: What do you get from a forgetful cow?

A: Milk of amnesia!

Q: What do you get from a grouchy cow?

A: Sour milk!

Q: What do you get from a cold cow?

A: Ice cream!

Q: What do you call a cow in an earthquake?

A: A milkshake!

Q: What do you call a cow who gives no milk?

A: An udder failure!

Q: What do you get from a brown cow?

A: Chocolate milk!

Q: What do you call a twitching cow?

A: Beef jerky!

Q: What do you call a sleeping bull?

A: A bull-dozer!

Q: How do you stop a bull from charging?

A: Take away his credit card!

Q: Why do cows wear bells?

A: Their horns don't work!

Q: What do you call a royal cow?

A: Cowntess!

Q: What was the first animal in space?

A: The cow that jumped over the moon!

Q: Why did the cow cross the road?

A: To get to the udder side!

Q: Where do cows eat lunch?

A: At the calf-eteria!

Q: What happens when you talk to a cow?

A: It goes in one ear and out the udder!

Q: Why do cows lie down when it rains?

A: To keep each udder dry!

Q: What do surfing cows say?

A: "Cowabunga!"

Q: What did the mommy cow say to her calf?

A: "Go to sleep—it's pasture bedtime!"

Criss Cross

What do you get if you cross one thing with another? Let's find out!

Q: What do you get if you cross a duck and an avocado?

A: Quackamole!

Q: What do you get if you cross a sheep and a kangaroo?

A: A woolly good jumper!

Q: What do you get if you cross a sheep and a bee?

A: Baa humbug!

Q: What do you get if you cross a bunny with Chinese food?

A: Hop suey!

Q: What do you get if you cross a dinosaur and a pig?

A: Jurassic pork!

Q: What do you get when you cross a penguin and a crocodile?

A: I don't know, but don't try to straighten its bow tie!

Q: What do you get if you cross a chicken and a dog?

A: Pooched eggs!

Q: What do you get when you cross a thief and an alligator?

A: A crookodile!

Q: What do you get if you cross a sheep and Superman?

A: The Man of Steel Wool!

Q: What do you get if you cross an angry sheep and a grumpy cow?

A: An animal that's in a baaaad mooooood!

Q: What do you get when you cross a dog and a library?

A: A hush puppy!

Q: What do you get when you cross a dog with a bar of soap?

A: A shampoodle!

Q: What do you get if you cross a bird with a thunderstorm?

A: Fowl weather!

What do you get if you cross a cocker spaniel, a poodle, and a rooster?

A: Cockerpoodledoo!

Q: What do you get if you cross a duck with breakfast?

A: Quacker Oats!

Q: What do you get when you cross a fish with an elephant?

A: Swimming trunks!

Q: What do you get if you cross ducks with fireworks?

A: Firequackers!

Q: What do you get if you cross an owl with a detective?

A: A who-done-it!

Q: What do you get if you cross a cat with a parrot?

A: A carrot!

Q: What do you get if you cross a chicken and a cow?

A: Roost beef!

Q: What do you get if you cross a kangaroo with an alien?

A: A Mars-upial!

Q: What do you get when you cross Moby Dick and a TV game show?

A: Whale of Fortune!

Q: What do you get if you cross a lamb and a rocket?

A: A space sheep!

Pig Out

The pigs deserve a turn to hog the spotlight. These jokes will have you squealing with laughter!

Q: What do you call a pig with no legs?

A: A groundhog!

Q: What do you call a pig stuck in a bush?

A: A hedgehog!

Q: Where do pigs keep their money?

A: In the piggy bank!

Q: Why shouldn't you tell secrets to pigs?

A: They always squeal!

Q: Did you hear about the pig who won the lottery?

A: He was filthy rich!

Q: Why shouldn't you share your bed with a pig?

A: They always hog the covers!

Q: What do you call two pigs who write letters to each other?

A: Pigpen pals!

Q: Why did the pig become an actor?

A: He was a real ham!

Q: Where do athletic pigs go?

A: To the Olympigs!

Q: Why was the pig arrested?

A: He was a pig-pocket!

Q: What do you get if you play tug-of-war with a pig?

A: Pulled pork!

Q: What happened when the pig pen broke?

A: The pigs had to use a pencil!

Q: Did you hear about the pig who lost his voice?

A: He was disgruntled!

Q: How do you fit more pigs on your farm?

A: Build a sty-scraper!

Q: Why did the pig stop sun-bathing?

A: He was so hot, he was bacon!

Q: What do you call a pig that's no fun?

A: A boar!

Q: How do pigs send secret messages?

A: With invisible oink!

Q: Which US president do pigs like best?

A: AbraHAM Lincoln!

Q: How do pigs clean their clothes?

A: They do a load of hogwash!

Q: What do you call a pig who does karate?

A: A pork chop!

Q: Where do pigs leave their cars?

A: In the porking lot!

Q: What kind of vehicles do pigs drive?

A: Pig-up trucks!

Q: What do piglets do after school?

A: Their hamwork!

Q: What do pigs dress up as on Halloween?

A: Frankenswine!

Feeling Sheepish

These jokes are so BAAd, they're good. Get the giggles with these silly sheep.

Q: If a dog has fleas, what does a sheep have?

A: Fleece!

Q: What do you call a sheep with no legs and no head?

A: A cloud!

Q: How many sheep do you need to make a sweater?

A: None! Sheep can't knit!

Q: **Which farm animal is the quietest?**
A: A shhhhheep!

Q: **What do sheep wear to work?**
A: Ewe-niforms!

Q: **Where do sheep get their hair cut?**
A: At the baa-baa shop!

Q: Why did the sheep get pulled over by the police?

A: She made an illegal ewe turn!

Q: What do sheep say to each other on Valentine's Day?

A: I love ewe!

Q: What do you call a dancing sheep?

A: A baa-llerina!

Q: Which fruit do sheep like best?

A: Baa-nanas!

Q: What do you call a chocolate-covered sheep?

A: A candy baa!

Straight from the Horse's Mouth

Horses can be hilarious, and these jokes prove it!

Q: How long should a horse's legs be?

A: Just long enough to reach the ground!

Q: What do racehorses eat?

A: Fast food!

Q: Where do horses shop?

A: Old Neigh-vy!

Q: Did you hear about the horse with a bad attitude?

A: He always said "Neigh!"

Q: What do you call a horse that lives next door?

A: A neigh-bor!

Q: What do horses do at bedtime?

A: They hit the hay!

Q: What do you call a really long horse race?

A: A mare-athon!

Q: What is a horse's favorite sport?

A: Stable tennis!

Q: Which street do horses live on?

A: Mane Street!

Q: What kind of horses go out after dark?

A: Nightmares!

Q: Why did the horse talk with food in its mouth?

A: It had poor stable manners!

Q: A man rode his horse to town on Friday. The next day he rode back on Friday. How is this possible?

A: The horse's name was Friday.

Q: Why did the horse cross the road?

A: Somebody shouted "hay"!

Q: What did the mommy horse say to her naughty pony?

A: "Quit foaling around!"

Goofy Donkeys

Chuckle along with these mischievous mules.

Q: If a grown-up donkey is a burro, what is a baby donkey?

A: A burrito!

Q: What do donkeys send out at Christmas?

A: Mule-tide greetings!

Q: What do you call a mule with one leg?

A: A wonky donkey!

Q: What party game do mules hate?

A: Pin the tail on the donkey!

Under the Weather

The animals are feeling a little under the weather. Help them out by spreading some good-natured grins!

Q: Why did the pony have a sore throat?

A: It was a little horse!

Q: Where did the duck go when he was sick?

A: To the duck-tor!

Q: What did the horse say when it tripped?

A: "I've fallen and I can't giddyup!"

Q: Why was the horse running a temperature?

A: He had hay fever!

Q: When do sheep go to the doctor?

A: When they feel baaaaad!

Q: Where do horses go when they're sick?

A: The horse-pital!

Q: What do you give a pig with a rash?

A: Oinkment!

Q: Did you hear that all of Farmer Joe's pigs are sick?

A: It's a real snoutbreak!

Q: What if all the pigs in the world got sick?

A: It would be a hamdemic!

Q: How do you get a sick pig to the hospital?

A: In a hambulance!

Q: Why did the cow switch doctors?

A: She wanted an udder opinion!

Q: Who takes care of the animals when the farmer is sick?

A: The farmacist!

Q: What do you give a sick horse?

A: Cough stirrup!

Q: Why did the bee go to the doctor?

A: Because he had hives!

On Vacation

After all these jokes, the animals have earned some rest. Let's go with them on a well-deserved vacation.

Q: Where did the goats go on vacation?

A: The Galapagoat Islands!

Q: Where did the cows go on vacation?

A: Moo York City!

Q: Where did the pigs go on vacation?

A: Yellowstone Pork!

Q: Where did the chickens go on vacation?

A: San Di-egg-o!

Q: Where did the sheep go on vacation?

A: The Baahamas!

Q: Where did the ducks go on vacation?

A: North Duckota!

Q: Where did the horses go on vacation?

A: Maine!

Q: What has four legs, a trunk, and sunglasses?

A: An elephant on vacation!

It's a Fine Feathered World

The bird world is a funny place, and these jokes prove it. Get ready, because laughter is about to take flight!

Q: How many cans does it take to make a bird?

A: Two cans!

Q: Where does a bird have the most feathers?

A: On the outside!

Q: What type of movies do birds like best?

A: Chick flicks!

Q: What do doctors give sick birds?

A: Tweetment!

Q: What do you get if you kiss a bird?

A: A peck on the cheek!

Q: What books do owls like?

A: Hoo-dunits!

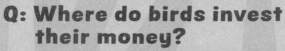

Q: What do you call a bird in the winter?

A: A brrrrr-d!

Q: Where do birds invest their money?

A: In the stork market!

Q: What is black and white and black and white and black and white?

A: A penguin rolling down a hill!

Q: **What is black and white and red all over?**

A: A penguin with a sunburn!

Q: **Why are geese such rude drivers?**

A: They're always honking!

Q: **What language does a goose speak?**

A: Portu-geese!

Q: **What sound does a bird's phone make?**

A: Wing, wing!

Why, Oh Why?

Why, oh why are these jokes so goofy? Only the birds know for sure!

Q: Why did the police arrest the bird?

A: They suspected it of fowl play!

Q: Why did the little bird get in trouble at school?

A: He was caught tweeting on a test!

Q: Why do birds fly south for the winter?

A: It's too far to walk!

Q: Why did the bird sit on the ax?

A: To hatchet!

Q: Why do storks stand on one leg?

A: They would fall over if they lifted the other one!

Q: Why do hummingbirds hum?

A: They don't know the words!

Q: Why did the owl say "Tweet, tweet"?

A: She didn't give a hoot!

Q: What do you call a bird that's always hitting its head?

A: Duck!

Q: Why did the bargain hunter buy a bird?

A: It was really cheep!

Q: Why do birds stretch before they exercise?

A: They need to worm up!

Q: What do you call a wood-pecker with no beak?

A: A headbanger!

Q: Why did the crow use the telephone?

A: He wanted to make a long-distance caw!

Q: Where does a peacock go when it loses its tail?

A: The re-tail store!

Q: Where do parrots go to become famous actors?

A: Pollywood!

Q: What kind of math do owls like?

A: Owlgebra!

Q: What do you call a bird that sticks to a sweater?

A: Vel-crow!

Q: What bird is with you at every meal?

A: A swallow!

Q: What's smarter than a talking parrot?

A: A spelling bee!

Did You Hear?

Did you hear about these silly birds?

Q: Did you hear about the turkey with a swearing problem?

A: He always used fowl language!

Q: Did you hear about the bird who was always looking in the mirror?

A: He was chicken himself out!

Q: Did you hear about the bird who didn't know how to do his job?

A: He just winged it!

Q: Did you hear about the chicken who joined a band?

A: He had his own drumsticks!

Q: Did you hear about the upset bird?

A: She got her feathers ruffled!

Q: How does a bird with a broken wing land safely?

A: With its sparrowchute!

Q: What do you call a parrot that flies away?

A: A Polly-gon!

What Kind of Bird?

What kind of bird makes you giggle? All of them, when you tell these goofy jokes!

Q: What kind of bird do you find in prison?

A: A jailbird!

Q: What kind of bird doesn't need a comb?

A: A bald eagle!

Q: What kind of bird can lift heavy weights?

A: A crane!

Q: What kind of bird is always out of breath?

A: A puffin!

Q: What kind of bird opens doors?

A: A key-wi!

Q: What kind of bird is always sad?

A: A bluebird!

Q: What kind of bird makes fun of other birds?

A: A mockingbird!

Q: What kind of bird flies over bays?

A: A bagel!

Q: What vegetable to geese like to eat?

A: Aspara-goose!

All About Chickens

These jokes will have you clucking with delight.

Q: Which day of the week do chickens hate most?

A: Fry-day!

Q: How did the chicken wake up?

A: It had an alarm cluck!

Q: How do chickens bake cakes?

A: From scratch!

Q: What do you call an odd chicken?

A: Peck-uliar!

Q: How did the chicken mail a letter to her friend?

A: In a hen-velope!

Q: What do you call a haunted chicken?

A: A poultry-geist!

Q: What time do chickens go to lunch?

A: Twelve o'cluck!

Q: What do you call a chicken that tells jokes?

A: A comedi-hen!

Q: What do chicken families do for fun?

A: They go on peck-nics!

Q: How do chickens dance?

A: Chick to chick!

Q: If a rooster laid an egg on a roof, which way would the egg roll?

A: Neither. Roosters don't lay eggs!

Q: What did the naughty chicken lay?

A: A deviled egg!

Q: What do you call a scared bird?

A: A chicken!

Crossing the Road

Why did the chicken cross the road? These jokes shed some light on this burning question.

Q: Why did the chicken cross the road?

A: To get to the other side!

Q: Why did the rooster cross the road?

A: To cockadoodle doo something!

Q: Why did the gum cross the road?

A: It was stuck to the chicken's foot!

Q: Why did half a chicken cross the road?

A: To get to its other side!

Q: Why did the sneaky chicken cross the road twice?

A: He was a double crosser!

Q: Why did the turkey cross the road?

A: It was the chicken's day off!

Q: Why did the rubber chicken cross the road?

A: She wanted to stretch her legs!

Q: Why did the turkey cross the road?

A: To prove he wasn't chicken!

Q: Why did the chicken cross the basketball court?

A: The referee was calling fowls!

Q: Why did the chicken cross the playground?

A: To get to the other slide!

Q: Why did the chicken cross the beach?

A: To get to the other tide!

Q: Why did the chicken cross the clothing store?

A: To get to the other size!

Q: Why did the chicken cross the amusement park?

A: To get to the other ride!

Q: What was the farmer doing on the other side of the road?

A: Catching all the chickens!

These Jokes Are Real Turkeys

Gobble, gobble! Here are some turkey jokes to share with your friends. They're gonna eat 'em up!

Q: What key won't open any doors?

A: A turkey!

Q: What happened when the turkey got into a fight?

A: He got the stuffing knocked out of him!

Q: What did the turkey eat on Thanksgiving?

A: Nothing—he was already stuffed!

Q: Why do turkeys have bad table manners?

A: Because they always gobble, gobble!

Q: What do dizzy turkeys do?

A: Wobble, wobble!

Q: Where do turkeys go to dance?

A: The Butterball!

Q: What do limping turkeys do?

A: Hobble, hobble!

Q: What is a turkey's favorite website?

A: Google, Google!

Q: What do you call leftover turkey?

A: A sandwich!

Q: How do you make a turkey float?

A: Root beer, a scoop of ice cream, and a turkey!

Q: What is a turkey's favorite dessert?

A: Peach gobbler!

Q: What do you call a turkey the day after Thanksgiving?

A: Lucky!

Q: What does a turkey drink from?

A: A gobble-et!

Duck!

You'd better duck! These jokes are coming at you fast!

Q: What time do ducks wake up?

A: At the quack of dawn!

Q: What do you call a crate of ducks?

A: A box of quackers!

Q: What steals your stuff while you're taking a bath?

A: A robber ducky!

Q: What do ducks watch on TV?

A: Duckumentaries!

Q: What happens when you tell a duck a joke?

A: He quacks up!

Q: Why couldn't the duck find her egg?

A: She mislaid it!

Q: What did the duck say to the waiter?

A: "Put it on my bill!"

Under the Sea

Explore an ocean of jokes with funny finned friends!

Q: How do you make an octopus laugh?
A: You give it ten-tickles!

Q: What fish loves the nighttime?
A: A starfish!

Q: What do you need to weigh a fish?
A: Nothing—it has its own scales!

Q: What do fish take to stay healthy?
A: Vitamin sea!

Q: What did the Cinderella fish wear to the ball?

A: Glass flippers!

Q: How is a shark like a computer?

A: They both have mega-bites!

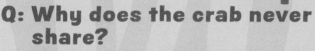

Q: Why does the crab never share?

A: Because he's shellfish!

Q: What's the difference between a fish and a piano?

A: You can't tuna fish!

Q: What do killer whales love to listen to?

A: Orca-stras!

Q: What kind of fish loves peanut butter?

A: A jellyfish!

Q: How do you make a goldfish old?
A: Take away the "g"!

Q: Why did the crab blush?
A: Because it saw the ocean's bottom!

Q: How do you communicate with a fish?
A: Drop it a line!

Q: What is a shark's favorite game?
A: Swallow the leader!

Q: What do fish use for money?
A: Sand dollars!

Q: Why are fish so smart?
A: Because they live in schools!

Q: Why does an octopus win in a fight?

A: Because it's well-armed!

Q: Why do fish live in salt water?

A: Because pepper makes them sneeze!

Q: What do you call octopuses that look exactly the same?

A: Itenticle!

Gone to the Dogs

These jokes are doggone funny!

Q: What kind of dog can tell you the time?

A: A watch dog!

Q: What do you call a dog with a fever?

A: A hot dog!

Q: What is a dog's least favorite store?

A: The flea market!

Q: What do you call a dog magician?

A: A labracadabrador!

Q: Why did the dog cross the road?

A: To get to the "barking" lot!

Q: What do you call a frozen dog?

A: A pupsicle!

Q: What is a dog's favorite vegetable?

A: "Collie-flower"!

Q: What is a dog's favorite state?

A: New Yorkie!

Q: What is the only kind of dog you can eat?

A: A hot dog!

Q: What is a dog's favorite pizza topping?

A: Pupperoni!

Q: What do you call a fat dog?

A: Husky!

Q: How is a dog like a telephone?

A: It has collar ID!

Q: Why did the dog have to pay a fine?

A: He got a barking ticket!

Q: How do you get a dog to stop digging in the garden?

A: Take away his shovel!

Just Kitten Around

Cat-ch some laughs with funny felines!

Q: What kind of cat would you not want to play a game with?

A: A cheetah!

Q: What is a cat's favorite treat?

A: Mice krispies!

Q: What is a cat's favorite color?

A: Purr-ple!

Q: What is a cat's favorite song?

A: "Three Blind Mice"!

Q: What do you call a kitten who counterfeits money?

A: A copycat!

Q: Why are cats bad storytellers?

A: Because they only have one tale!

Q: Which side of a cat has the most hair?

A: The outside!

Q: Which kind of cat can jump higher than a house?

A: All of them. Houses can't jump!

Q: What does a kitten become after it's one year old?

A: Two years old!

Q: What kind of cars do cats drive?

A: Catillacs!

Q: How do you keep a cat in suspense?

A: I'll tell you later . . .

A Llama Laughs!

Get ready to Llol with llots of llama jokes!

Q: Why were the llamas in a fight?

A: There was a llama drama!

Q: What do you call a super-fast llama?

A: A llama-ghini!

Q: What do you get if you bring a llama to a party?

A: A wooly good time!

Q: What do call a llama who can't do math?

A: A no prob-llama!

Q: What do you call a gigantic llama?

A: A wooly mammoth!

Q: What does a llama write on a valentine?

A: "Wool you be mine?"

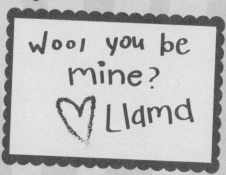

Q: What's a llama's favorite food?

A: Llama beans!

Q: What's a llama's favorite car?

A: A llamasine!

Q: What do you get when you cross a llama with pasta?

A: Llamasagna!

Q: What do you get when you cross a llama with the end of the world?

A: Llamageddon!

Q: What's a llama's favorite drink?

A: Llamanade!

Funny Bunny

These ridiculous rabbit jokes are hopping hilarious!

Q: Where do bunnies go for breakfast?

A: IHOP!

Q: Where do rabbits go after their wedding?

A: On their bunnymoon!

Q: What do you call a rabbit with fleas?

A: Bugs Bunny!

Q: What did the rabbit say to the carrot?

A: "It's been nice gnawing you!"

Q: How do rabbits travel?
A: By hareplane!

Q: What is a rabbit's favorite kind of music?
A: Hip-hop!

Q: How can you tell which rabbits are getting old?
A: Look for the gray hares!

Q: What do you call a line of rabbits walking backward?
A: A receding hare line!

Q: What is a bunny's motto?
A: Don't be worry, be hoppy!

Q: How do you catch a unique rabbit?
A: Unique up on it!

Q: How do you know carrots are good for your eyes?
A: Because you never see rabbits wearing glasses!

Amusing Animals

If it moos, barks, snorts, or trumpets, it's probably hilarious in some way! Check out these funny jokes about the always-amusing animal kingdom.

Q: What sound do porcupines make when they kiss?

A: Ouch!

Q: Did you hear about the grizzly who wouldn't wear shoes?

A: He didn't see the point. He'd still have bear feet!

Q: Why can't you shock a bunch of elephants?

A: They've herd it all!

Q: What is as big as an elephant but weighs nothing?

A: The elephant's shadow!

Q: Why did the baby elephant need a new suitcase for her vacation?

A: She only had a little trunk!

Q: Why did the elephant quit the circus?

A: It was tired of working for peanuts!

Q: What animal is the best at baseball?

A: A bat!

Q: What time is it when an elephant sits on your bed?

A: Time to get a new bed!

Q: How do you stop an elephant from charging?

A: Take away his credit card!

Q: What do you call an exploding monkey?

A: A baboom!

Q: What do you call an angry monkey?

A: Furious George!

Q: What do you call a deer with no eyes?

A: No-eye-deer!

Q: What do you call a deer with flashlights for eyes?

A: A bright-eye-deer!

Q: What do you call a deer that costs a dollar?

A: A buck!

Q: Did you hear about the penguin who drove a race car?

A: He always got pole position!

Q: What did the leopard say after finishing dinner?

A: "That hit the spot!"

Q: What happens when a frog's car breaks down?

A: It gets toad away!

Q: What is the difference between an alligator and a crocodile?

A: One you will see later, one you will see in a while!

Q: What do you call a crocodile with GPS?

A: A navi-gator!

Q: What is the first thing a bat learns in school?

A: The alpha-bat!

Q: What did the judge say when the skunk walked into the courtroom?

A: "Odor in the court!"

Q: What do you call an untidy hippo?

A: A hippopota-mess!

Q: What's a crocodile's favorite drink?

A: Gator-ade!

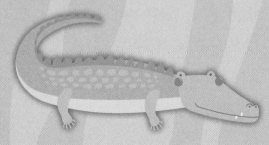

Q: Why isn't a koala an actual bear?

A: It doesn't meet the koalafications!

Q: What do you call a bear with no teeth?

A: A gummy bear!

Q: How much money does a skunk have?

A: One scent!

Q: How many skunks does it take to make a stink?

A: A phew!

Q: Why don't bears like fast food?

A: They can't catch it!

Q: What do you call bears with no ears?

A: B!

Q: Where does a 600-pound gorilla sit?

A: Anywhere he wants!

Q: What do you call a gorilla wearing earmuffs?

A: Anything you like—he can't hear you.

Q: How do you catch a squirrel?

A: Climb a tree and act like a nut!

Q: Did you hear about the lion who ate the clown?

A: He felt funny!

Q: How do camels disguise themselves in the desert?

A: They use camelflauge!

Q: Did you hear about the laid-back polar bear?

A: He was just chilling out!

Q: Why do panda bears like old movies?

A: Because they're in black and white!

Q: What do polar bears sing at birthday parties?

A: "Freeze a jolly good fellow!"

Q: What's a polar bear's favorite food?

A: Ice-bergers!

Q: Why did the giraffe get bad grades in school?

A: His head was always in the clouds!

Q: What is a frog's favorite year?

A: Leap year!

Q: How does a seal make pancakes?

A: With its flippers!

Q: What do you call a groundhog who eats too much?

A: A roundhog!

Q: Why do mother kangaroos hate rainy days?

A: Because their kids have to play inside!

Q: Why are giraffes so slow to apologize?

A: It takes them a long time to swallow their pride!

Q: What's gray and has four legs and a trunk?

A: A mouse on vacation!

Q: Where does a mouse park his boat?

A: The hickory dickory dock!

Q: Why was the mouse afraid of the water?

A: The catfish!

Q: How is a baby bird like its dad?

A: It's a chirp off the old block!

Q: What do you call a mouse after it takes a bath?

A: Squeaky clean!

Q: How does a lion greet another animal?

A: "Pleased to eat you!"

Q: What did the momma buffalo say to her son before he went to school?

A: "Bison!"

Creepy, Crawly, and Comical

Bugs, snakes, spiders, and other creepy-crawly critters are icky, scary...and hilarious! Turn your shivers into laughs with these silly jokes!

Q: Who always comes to a picnic but is never invited?

A: Ants!

Q: What do you call a fly without wings?

A: A walk!

Q: Why didn't the butterfly go to the dance?

A: Because it was a mothball!

Q: Why is a bee's hair always sticky?

A: Because it uses a honey comb!

Q: How do bees get to school?

A: On the school buzz!

Q: What does a bee say when it returns to the hive?

A: Honey, I'm home!

Q: Where do bees sit?

A: On their bee-hinds!

Q: How do spiders communicate?

A: Through the World Wide Web!

Q: What's worse than finding a worm in your apple?

A: Finding half a worm!

Q: Did you hear about the bed bugs who met in the mattress?

A: They got married in the spring!

Q: What do you get when you cross a snake with dessert?

A: A pie-thon!

Q: What do you do when two snails start a fight?

A: You just let them slug it out!

Q: What has four wheels and flies?

A: A garbage truck!

Q: Why are snakes hard to fool?

A: You can't pull their leg!

Q: What did the snake do when he got upset?

A: He threw a hissy fit!

Q: Why are spiders like tops?

A: They're always spinning!

Q: How do fleas travel?

A: They itch-hike!

Q: Why did the fly fly?

A: Because the spider spied 'er!

Q: How do you make a glowworm happy?

A: Remove his tail—he'll be de-lighted!

Q: Which snakes are found on cars?

A: Windshield vipers!

Q: **How do snakes put their babies to bed?**

A: With a good-night hiss!

Q: **What is a snake's favorite subject in school?**

A: Hiss-tory!

Q: **What do you call two spiders who just got married?**

A: Newlywebs!

Q: **How many ants does it take to rent a house?**

A: Ten ants!

Q: **What do you call a dead fly?**

A: A flew!

Real Winners

Q: What do you call a pig that won the lottery?

A: Filthy rich!

Q: Did you hear about the yak who bought a winning lottery ticket?

A: He hit the yak-pot!

Q: Did you hear about the frog that won $1,000?

A: He was toad-ally excited!

Q: Why do rabbits play the lottery?

A: They want to be million-hares!

Delightful Dinosaurs

These hilarious jokes will never go extinct!

Q: What do you call a sleeping dinosaur?

A: A dino-snore!

Q: What kind of dinosaur knows a lot of words?

A: A thesaurus!

Q: What kind of dinosaur gets into accidents?

A: Tyrannosaurus wrecks!

Q: What do you get when you cross a dinosaur with fireworks?

A: Dino-mite!

Q: What does a T. rex eat?

A: Anything it wants!

Q: What do you call a dinosaur who never gives up?

A: A try-try-try-ceratops!

Q: What do you call dinosaur police?

A: Tricera-cops!

Q: Why do dinosaurs eat their food raw?

A: Because they don't know how to cook!

Q: What do you get if you cross a triceratops with a kangaroo?

A: A tricera-hops!

Q: Where do triceratops sit?
A: On their tricera-bottoms!

Q: What should you do if you find a T. rex in your bedroom?
A: Run!

Q: Why did the T. rex need a Band-Aid?
A: He had a dino-sore!